Jane Addams
A Photo Biography

by John Riley, M.Ed.

First Biographies
an Imprint of Morgan Reynolds, Inc.

Greensboro

Jane Addams: A Photo Biography

Copyright © 2000 by John Riley

All rights reserved.
This book, or parts thereof, may not be reproduced in any form except by written consent of the publisher. For information write:
Morgan Reynolds, Inc., 620 S. Elm St., Suite 384
Greensboro, North Carolina 27406 USA

Photo credits: Jane Addams Memorial Collection (JAMC negatives 613, 2, 64, 850, 9, 495, and 146) Special Collections, University Library, University of Illinois at Chicago.

Library of Congress Cataloging-in-Publication Data

Riley, John
 Jane Addams : a photo-biography / by John Riley.-- 1st ed.
  p. cm.
 Includes bibliographical references (p.) and index.
 Summary: Describes the life and work of the woman whose work to help the poor in Chicago and around the world won her the Nobel Peace Prize.
 ISBN 1-883846-61-7
 1. Addams, Jane, 1860-1935--Juvenile literature. 2. Addams, Jane, 1860-1935--Pictoral works. 3. Women social workers--United States--Biography--Juvenile literature. 4. Women social reformers--United States--Biography--Juvenile literature. [1. Addams, Jane, 1860-1935. 2. Social workers. 3. Women--Biography. 4. Nobel Prizes--Biography.] I. Title.

HV28.A35 .R56 2000
361.92--dc21
[B]

99-089221

Printed in the United States of America

First Edition

Table of Contents

Helping Others 5

Childhood 7

Moves to Chicago 9

Hull House 11

Spreading the Message 13

Politics 15

World War I 17

Nobel Peace Prize 19

Last Years 21

Timeline 22

Words to Know 22

Further Reading 23

Websites 23

Places to Write 24

Index 24

Boldface words are defined in **Words to Know**.

Helping Others

Jane Addams wanted to help people. She fed those who had no food. She taught people how to read.

Jane also spoke out against war. She wrote books and gave speeches. Her dream was for the world to live in peace.

Today Jane is remembered as a kind and good person. She wanted people to be generous and to help others.

Jane Addams worked to make the world a better place.

Childhood

Jane Addams was born on September 6, 1860. She was born in Cedarville, Illinois.

Jane liked to fish and hike and to read books. She finished high school when she was 16 years old. Then she went to college.

Jane visited London, England, in 1881. There were thousands of hungry and homeless people in London. "Does anyone help these people?" she wondered.

Jane grew up in this house in Cedarville, Illinois.

Moves to Chicago

Jane moved to Chicago, Illinois. People came from all over the world to live in Chicago. They were called **immigrants**. The immigrants lived in areas called **slums**. Many needed food and clothes. Some were homeless.

Jane wanted to help the immigrants. She asked others to help. Most people said that they did not have time.

Many poor immigrants lived in Chicago.

Hull House

Jane bought a house near the slums. She called it Hull House. The people who worked in Hull House were called **volunteers**.

The volunteers cooked and served free food. They helped people find jobs and houses.

Sometimes it was dangerous living in Hull House. Jane refused to be afraid. She had too much work to do.

Jane opened Hull House to help poor people.

Spreading the Message

Jane asked the rich people for money to help the poor people.

Jane believed that children should not work in factories. Workers should earn enough money to have a home. Jane wrote a book about her beliefs.

People came to Hull House from many different places. Jane asked them to go home and help the poor in their cities.

Jane did not want children to work in factories.

HEADQUARTERS NATIONAL ASSOCIATI
OPPOSED TO
WOMAN SUFFRAGE

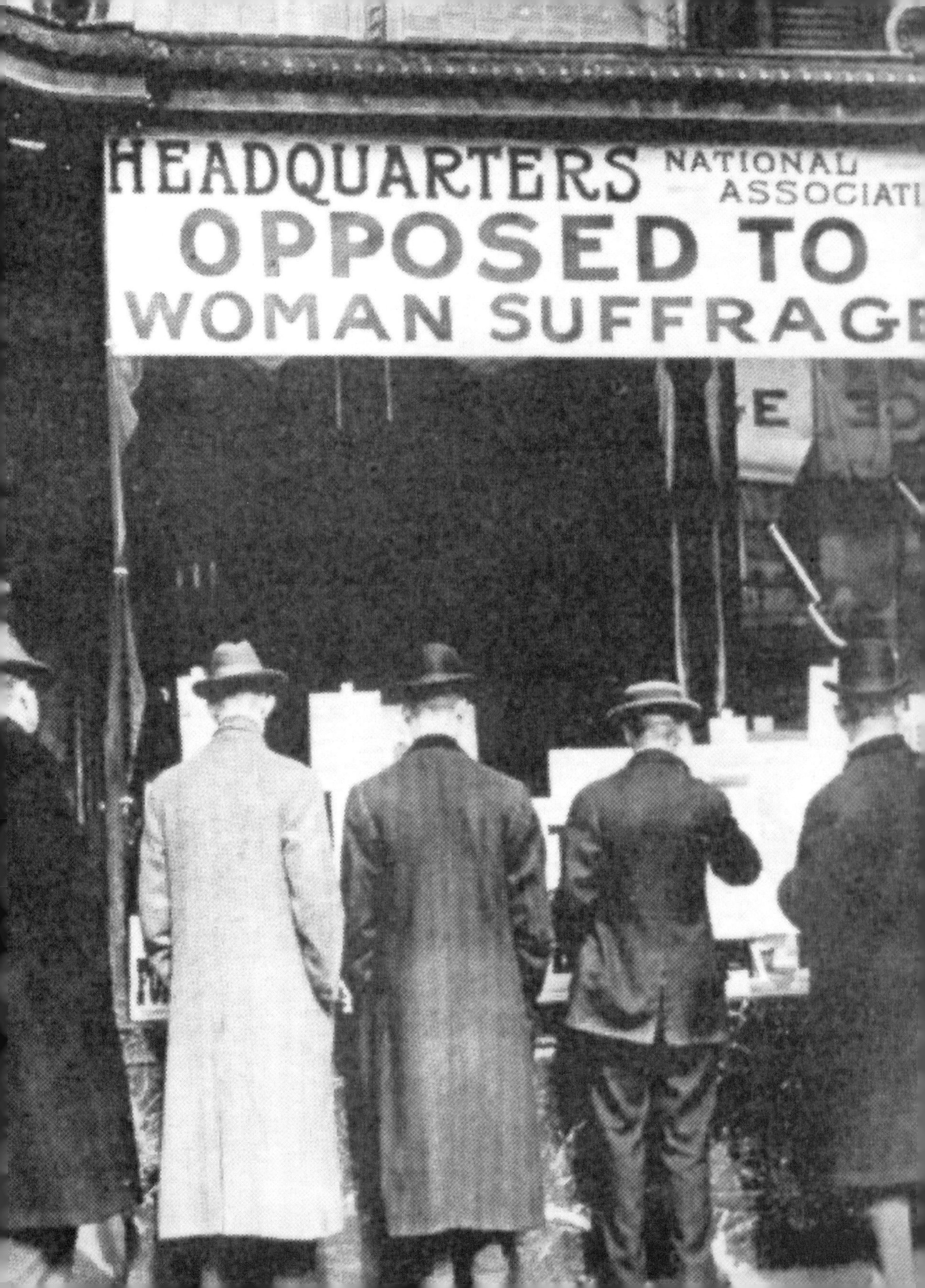

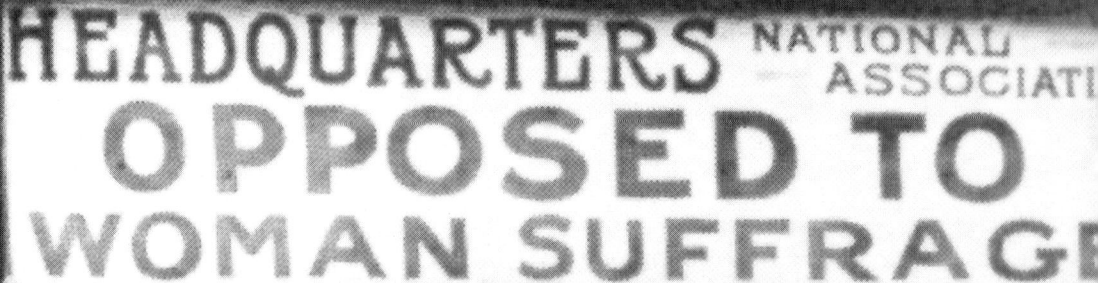

Politics

Jane traveled and gave speeches. She visited the president.

Jane said that African Americans were not treated fairly. The laws should treat everyone the same.

Jane believed women should have the right to vote in elections. The right to vote is called **suffrage**.

Jane worked hard on these **issues**. In 1919 women were granted the right to vote.

Many people believed women should not vote.

World War I

World War I started in Europe in 1914. Jane traveled to Europe to stop the war.

Jane said that war did not solve problems. She said that war was the problem.

The United States fought the Germans in the war. Most Americans supported the war. Jane spoke out against it.

Jane worked for peace during World War I.

Nobel Peace Prize

World War I ended in 1918. Jane traveled to other parts of the world. She asked the rich countries to help the poor countries.

Jane won the Nobel Peace Prize in 1931. She was chosen from all the people in the world to win the prize.

The Nobel Peace Prize honored her work against war.

Jane believed children should have food, shelter, and education.

Last Years

In the 1930s millions of Americans had no jobs. These years are called the **Great Depression**.

Hull House fed hundreds of people. Jane worked very hard. She died on May 21, 1935. Thousands of people attended her funeral.

Jane Addams will be remembered for helping people. She said that everyone should be treated with kindness.

Jane Addams will be remembered for her kindness.

Timeline

1860—Born in Cedarville, Illinois, on September 6.
1881—Goes to London, England.
1889—Opens Hull House in Chicago, Illinois.
1918—Travels the U. S. helping people save food.
1931—Wins the Nobel Peace Prize.
1935—Dies in Chicago, Illinois.

Words to Know

Great Depression: [GRAYT de-PRE-shun] a period when people did not have jobs, beginning in 1929.
immigrants: [IM-uh-grants] people who move from one country to live in another country.
issues: [ISH-yoos] difficult problems that people try to find solutions for.
slums: [SLUMZ] poor areas of a city or town.
suffrage: [SUFF-redge] the right to vote.
volunteers: [voll-un-TEERS] people who work to help others, not for money.

Further Reading

Hovde, Jane. *Jane Addams*. Facts on File. New York, 1989.

Kittredge, Mary. *Jane Addams*. Chelsea House. New York, 1988.

Linn, James Weber. *Jane Addams, A Biography*. Greenwood. Westport, CT, 1980.

Websites

Jane Addams Hull-House Museum:
http://www.uic.edu/jaddams/hull/hull_house.html

Chicago Public Library:
http://cpl.lib.uic.edu/004chicago/timeline/hullhouse.html

Places to Write

Jane Addams' Hull-House Museum
The University of Illinois at Chicago
800 South Halsted Street
Chicago, Illinois 60607-7017
(312) 413-5353

Index

Cedarville, Illinois, 7
Chicago, Illinois, 9
Great Depression, 21
Hull House, 11, 13, 21
immigrants, 9
issues, 15
London, England, 7
Nobel Peace Prize, 19
slums, 9, 11
suffrage, 15
volunteers, 11
World War I, 17, 19